THE REAL TADZIO

THE REAL TADZIO

THOMAS MANN'S *DEATH IN VENICE*
AND THE BOY WHO INSPIRED IT

gilbert adair

CARROLL & GRAF PUBLISHERS
NEW YORK

THE REAL TADZIO

Carroll & Graf Publishers
An Imprint of Avalon Publishing Group Inc.
161 William Street, 16th Floor
New York, NY 10038

First Carroll & Graf edition 2003

Library of Congress Cataloging-in-Publication Data is available.

ISBN: 0-7867-1247-3

Printed in the United States of America
Distributed by Publishers Group West

As it is, in three days I won't see the boy anymore, will forget his face. But not the experience of my heart. He will join that gallery about which no literary history will speak.

THOMAS MANN, *Diary,* July 11, 1950

ON A DECEMBER afternoon in 1910 Thomas Mann treated his immediate family circle, his wife and elder brother, to a reading of a short work of fiction, 'The Fight Between Jappe and Do Escobar', which he had just that day completed. Mann, who was then in his mid-thirties, had been feeling as ill-humoured, as cantankerous, as irritably out of sorts, as one of his own neurotic protagonists. He had laid aside (temporarily, he assumed) a projected comic novel to which, as it transpired, he would return only at the very end of his life and which was first published in English, with the rather unwieldy title *Confessions of Felix Krull, Confidence Man: the Early Years*, in 1955. He had also been troubled, although less profoundly than might have been predicted, by the horrific death of his younger sister Carla. The garish circumstances of her suicide – she had swallowed, as Mann himself was later to write, with an unnerving absence of sibling warmth, 'enough potassium cyanide to kill a company of soldiers' – suggested that poor Carla had ceased to make too much of a distinction between her own life and the melodramas in which, as a hopelessly third-rate actress, she had tended to be cast.

Unable to channel his intellectual energies into any form of extended labour, Mann had quickly dashed off his new story after an unexpected encounter with a childhood friend, Count Vitzum von Eckstädt, revived memories of their schooldays together, memories which, as was almost invariably his custom, he sought at once to transmute into fiction.

'The Fight Between Jappe and Do Escobar' is a minor but perfectly achieved example of Mann's story-telling genius. It centres on an abortive fist-fight between two youths, a German and a Spaniard, ref-ereed by a somewhat equivocal dancing-master, Herr Knaak ('who picked up the edge of his frock-coat with his finger-tips, curtsied, cut capers, leaped suddenly into the air, where he twirled his toes before he came down again'), and observed by a third boy, a twelve-year-old English cherub named Johnny Bishop. This is how Mann pictures Johnny in his Sunday finery: 'He was far and away the best-dressed boy in town, distinctly aristocratic and elegant in his real English sailor suit with the linen collar, sailor's knot, laces, a silver whistle in his pocket and an anchor on the sleeves that narrowed round his wrists.' And here is Johnny on the beach, languorous and naked: 'He looked rather like a thin little cupid as he lay there, with his pretty, soft blond curls and his arms up over the narrow English head that rested on the sand.' In the light of what was to happen to its author a mere six months later, such a description of pubescent androgyny now seems eerily prescient.

In May of the following year, fretting over head-, stomach- and tooth-aches (he was a lifelong martyr to his teeth), still incapable of settling down to real work, Mann decided that what he needed was a long holiday in the sun. So, accompanied by wife Katia, who was also ailing, and brother Heinrich, a by no means negligible novelist in his own right even if his reputation had already been overshadowed by Thomas's precocious neo-Goethean aura (if ever a writer wore his learning lightly, it wasn't Thomas Mann: Brecht, his arch-enemy, would mischievously refer to him as the 'Starched Collar'), he left Germany to spend a few weeks on the island of Brioni, off the Dalmatian coast.

From the start this hoped-for sabbatical from the agonies of creation was plagued with distractions and dissatisfactions. The weather was cold and cheerless, none of the trio cared much for Brioni, and Thomas

Gilbert Adair

Thomas Mann, 1875 - 1955

was especially incensed to discover that an unbroken line of chalk cliffs rendered a pedestrian's access to the Mediterranean, for which he had a Northerner's thirst, virtually impossible. Worst of all was the hotel, albeit the island's finest. The Archduchess of Austria was of the company and protocol required even non-Austrians to rise to their feet as she entered the dining room, which she affected to do only after all the other guests were seated. It was an irksome and demeaning performance made the more exasperating by having to be gone through a second time once the meal was over.

On impulse the Manns elected to cut short their sojourn and travel onward to what was then, as it is today, by far the least disappointing tourist spot in Europe, gorgeous, gangrenous Venice, 'the incomparable, the fabulous, the like-nothing-else-on-earth', in Thomas's ecstatic phrase. At Pola they bought passage on a steamer, aboard which they were both amused and bemused to witness the antics of an elderly, goatish queen (in the homosexual sense of the word) who had contrived to ingratiate himself with a party of boisterous clerks out on an excursion: with his crudely dyed moustache and grotesquely rouged cheeks, he reminded them all of Herr Knaak (who also, intriguingly, pops up in one of the most perfect

of Mann's short stories, *Tonio Kröger*). A more dis-
quieting incident followed at the steamer's landing
stage. The Manns had duly transferred their luggage
to a gondola which would take them to the Lido, at
whose Grand Hôtel des Bains they had two adjoin-
ing rooms reserved. But their gondolier proved to
be a surly, incommunicative fellow who, although he
steered them skilfully enough, proved reluctant to stay
around to collect his fare when they disembarked. It
turned out that, having had his licence revoked, he had
been alarmed by the presence on the pier of a cluster of
harbour policemen.

Eventually, however, the three were installed in
the sumptuous Hôtel des Bains. And it was there, on
their first evening, as they lounged among the elegant,
cosmopolitan crowd waiting for the gong to be
rung for dinner, that Thomas's attention was drawn
to a nearby Polish family, which consisted, in the
momentary absence of the mother (who, like the
Archduchess of Austria, appears to have been an
adept of the delayed entrance), of three starchily out-
fitted daughters and one very young son. Amazingly,
this sailor-suited ephebe – of, to his connoisseur's eye,
near-supernatural physical beauty and grace – was the
very image, teased into life, of the Johnny Bishop
whom Mann had conjured up just six months before.

Panicked by a cholera alarm, uncannily as portrayed in the pages of the novella-to-be, the writer, his wife and brother hastily quit the Lido only a week after their arrival and renounced all notion of a holiday. Back home – or, rather, in his newly built summer villa in Bad Tölz in Upper Bavaria – Thomas at once began work on *Death in Venice*, taking one entire year, the twelve months between July 1911 and July 1912, to compose the seventy-odd pages of his novella about an ageing writer in febrile thrall to the ultimately fatal charm of a Polish adolescent. (I am assuming that no one reading this book will require any more detailed synopsis of Mann's plot.) It was first published, to wellnigh universal acclaim, in two successive 1912 numbers of the *Neue Rundschau* revue and thereafter in book form, with an initial print run of eight thousand copies, in February 1913. That edition sold out at once, and the novella has been, ever since, in one edition or another, one translation or another, an international bestseller, still the most popular and widely read of all Mann's fictions. In fact, almost before it appeared, its fortunate publisher, Samuel Fischer, had proclaimed, with pardonable hyperbole, its instantaneous 'enrolment into the history of humanity'.

In the years which followed the 1911 trip, when

Death in Venice would, as Fischer had foreseen, come to be recognised as one of the undisputed classics of contemporary European literature, Mann was not averse to acknowledging a debt to the sublime happenstance which had laid out before him, *in the correct order*, a sequence of narrative units which could scarcely have failed, even in lesser hands than his, to engender a masterpiece. Even now, nearly a century after the event, it is not generally realised, save to the many specialists of Mann's work and life, that virtually everything experienced by Gustav von Aschenbach in the novella, short of his premature death on the beach, had first happened to the author. Yet Mann never sought to camouflage just how little of a novelist's imaginative gifts had gone into this particular tale. More than once he admitted to the world that there *really* had been an effeminate, posturing fop, a gruff gondolier, an aristocratic Polish family and, of course, a beautiful boy. As he himself wrote:

> Nothing is invented in *Death in Venice*. The 'pilgrim' at the North Cemetery [*who makes a brief cameo appearance in the prelude to the story proper*], the dreary Pola boat, the grey-haired rake, the sinister gondolier, Tadzio and his family, the journey interrupted

by a mistake about the luggage, the cholera, the upright clerk at the travel bureau, the rascally ballad singer, all that and anything else you like, they were all there. I had only to arrange them when they showed at once and in the oddest way their capacity as elements of composition.

Or, again, of his fateful sojourn in Venice:

A series of curious circumstances and impressions combined with my subconscious search for something new to give birth to a productive idea, which then developed into the story *Death in Venice*. The tale as at first conceived was as modest as all the rest of my undertakings; I thought of it as an interlude to my work on the Krull novel.

Yet, surprisingly, in that self-same year of 1912, Mann was complaining to Fischer of the novella's 'errors and weaknesses' and describing it to his brother Heinrich as 'full of half-baked ideas and falsehoods'. (By one of several weird coincidences that are threaded through our story, Heinrich had made his own international reputation with a lurid account of another intellectual prostrated by an unworthy object of desire, the novel *Professor Unrat*, the tale of a sadistic schoolmaster

who falls flat on his face in love with a blowsily allu-
ring nightclub chanteuse. If no longer very much
read, it is recalled still as the basis for the 1930 film,
Josef Von Sternberg's *Der Blaue Engel*, or *The Blue
Angel*, which first dangled Marlene Dietrich before a
mesmerised world.) Had he been afforded the opportunity of writing *Death in Venice* over again, Thomas
insisted, he would have made it significantly less of a
'mystification'. And, indeed, as we have long known,
the reality is that, notwithstanding his claims to the
contrary – that the novella's narrative had simply and
magically unfolded before his eyes and that all he
had had to do was transcribe it from life, as though
taking dictation from God – he had been as eco-
nomical with the factual truth as the majority of his
fellow-novelists.

Since fiction and autobiography are distinct if frequently overlapping categories, there were of course,
as ever, a number of trivial divergences in *Death in
Venice* from what we now know to have happened on
the trip which inspired it. Aschenbach, for example,
is alone in Venice, Mann was accompanied by his
brother and wife (and, as is clear from her memoirs,
the complaisant Katia was well aware in what dir-
ection her husband's eyes would usually rove, not
excluding, in the later years of their married life,

towards his own strikingly good-looking son Klaus); Aschenbach has an estranged daughter, Mann was not yet a father; Aschenbach brazenly pursues Tadzio just about everywhere the boy goes, Mann (according, again, to Katia) attempted to restrain himself, to rein in his passion; and so on.

Even in his supposedly humble and self-depreciating statement of the 'curious circumstances and impressions' which led to the creation of *Death in Venice*, Mann could not resist dissembling, refashioning his material to make it appear more miraculous than it was in reality. The 'mistake about the luggage', for example, listed above among the elements transferred – verbatim, as it were – from life into fiction, involved only Heinrich's cases, neither Thomas's nor Katia's; the rumour of cholera emanated not from Venice itself but from as far away from the northeastern coast of Italy as Palermo; and, more crucially, even before writing *Death in Venice*, Mann had long mulled over the idea of a short story whose subject would be the catastrophic loss of dignity suffered by a great and mature artist infatuated by a very much younger object of his lust. Nor had he been considering just any great and mature artist. His protagonist was to have been Goethe himself, who, in his seventh decade, fell in love with (and even, unbelievably, proposed marriage to) the seventeen-year-old Ulrike von Levetzow. Like his brother, Mann, although something of a prude in his public self-presentation, was patently fascinated by the expression 'to fall in love', by the notion that love is something one *falls* into.

(Incidentally, the putative story, which he discarded once he had returned from Italy with his new narrative windfall, was to have had the faintly *Death-in-Venice*-ish title of *Goethe in Marienbad*.)

Of greater significance, though, were the liberties which he allowed himself to take with the character of Tadzio. In the first place, the boy's name was not Tadzio at all – or Thaddeus, for which 'Tadzio' is the diminutive – but Wladyslaw. This, at least, was probably not a deliberate subterfuge on Mann's part (when he set to work on the novella, he sought advice on spelling from a Polish-speaking acquaintance). What Aschenbach, his protagonist, hears on the Lido, when the other children start calling the Polish youth to play, is 'something like Adgio – or, often still, Adjiu, with a long-drawn-out *u* at the end'. And that is exactly what Mann himself would have heard, save that Adgio – or, correctly, Adzio – is, via 'Wladzio', short for 'Wladyslaw'.

Even more significantly, Adzio was not a youth but a child. Wladyslaw Moes – the real boy's real name –

was born in the second half of 1900, which means that, at the time of their encounter on the Lido, he whom Mann would complacently portray as 'a long-haired boy of about fourteen' was not quite eleven years old, a significant difference where approaching or receding puberty is concerned. Furthermore, although his older beach companion 'Jaschiu' (Mann's phonetic spelling of 'Jasio', the vocative form of the name 'Jas') also existed, and was called Jan Fudakowski, he was in reality Adzio's junior by a few months and therefore neither the 'sturdy lad with brilliantined black hair' of the novella nor, *a fortiori*, the muscular hunk, visibly in his late teens or even early twenties, of the film which Luchino Visconti adapted from it in 1971.

In fairness to Mann, it should be pointed out that, if he aged Tadzio by three years – if, to borrow the term used in the antique trade to define the deliberate, frequently fraudulent 'antiquation' of furniture, he 'distressed' him – then he took a far greater liberty with his own fictional surrogate. In 1911 Mann was thirty-six years old. As for the hero of *Death in Venice*, it is in the novella's second sentence that the reader learns that the once plain, von-less Gustav Aschenbach had officially earned the right to be addressed by the nobler moniker 'Gustav von

Aschenbach' only, as the text has it, 'since his fiftieth birthday'. Aschenbach is, then, older than fifty. He may well be, in fact, approaching sixty, and therefore by some twenty years Mann's senior.

How should we interpret the fact that Mann chose to alter the factual age, so to speak, of not one but both of these fictional characters? As part of a structural tactic whereby – it being absolutely crucial to the novella's meaning that Aschenbach be shown to be an artist at the very height of his literary renown – it became necessary, if the 'miraculous' parallels with the real incident were to be upheld, to add a few extra years to Tadzio's own age? Or, less generously, as a sneaky endeavour by Mann to underplay, even minimize, the not always latent eroticism of his story, in that the desire for a prepubescent boy on the part of a late-middle-aged man would stand a chance (back in 1911 if not necessarily today) of being regarded as less threateningly carnal than that of one in his thirties? Or simply as a ruefully ironic reflection of how old Mann actually *felt* when caught in the headlamps of the eleven-year-old Wladyslaw Moes's limpid gaze? Whichever, it was almost certainly these age differences to which he was alluding when he spoke of wishing to demystify his work.

Mann, of course, never did write *Death in Venice*

over again. Nor, ever more Olympian and aloof, did he trouble to ascertain who precisely was the little Polish boy on the beach of the Lido or what might have become of him. I, on the other hand, did.

What follows, however, is not a biography; it might more accurately be viewed as an extended, belated specimen of the biography's less garrulous cousin, the obituary. (When Wladyslaw Moes died in Warsaw in 1986, his passing went, to my knowledge, completely unacknowledged in English-language newspapers.) The obituary is a peculiar genre, if genre it is. What it necessarily omits is the bread-and-butter routine which makes up most of the relatively spartan diets of most existences, not excluding those of celebrities, the humdrum connective tissue of even the most interesting individual's quotidian round. 'Life,' as Alfred Jarry once said, 'is so *daily*.' Obituaries dispense with the *daily*, that same laundry-list *daily* in which modern biographies revel.

This text, too (or, rather, the section which follows) will dispense with the daily, offering the reader instead a miniaturised overview of the life of Wladyslaw Moes. It is a life, one might say, examined through the small end of a telescope, with few aspirations on my part to probe, analyse or even simply speculate on what might have been my subject's mindset. It is one, too, that I juxtapose with that of Mann's Tadzio. For the lives of certain especially memorable literary (and, for that matter, cinematic) characters do not come to an end with the turning of the last pages of the books in which they began. Like Proust's Baron Charlus, Kafka's Joseph K, Fitzgerald's Jay Gatsby, Isherwood's Sally Bowles, Nabokov's Lolita, like so many others, Mann's single most famous creation has transcended the prose in which he was once canonically anchored and now floats, free and untrammelled, in an aquarium of folk myth and memory. Which is why, as fascinated by Mann's Tadzio as Mann himself was by the real Adzio, I decided that I would find out what happened to each of them after their paths crossed, as it were, during that Venetian summer of 1911.

***

In fact, bizarre as it may seem, little Adzio grew up in Poland as ignorant of, and indifferent to, the role which he had unwittingly played in Mann's masterpiece as, it appears, was the entire Moes family. The novella was almost immediately translated into most European languages, including Polish; yet it was not until twelve years later, in 1924, when Wladyslaw Moes was in his own early twenties, that one of his cousins finally read *Death in Venice*. Taken aback by the story's references to an aristocratic Polish family staying at the Hôtel des Bains, to the amusingly vulgar musicians who had been hired to entertain the resident clientele and the insidious rumours of cholera which had started to circulate through the city, taken most aback by the narrative premise of an elderly voyeur entranced by the spectacle, on the beach of the Lido, of two extremely personable young boys at play, boys whose nicknames, moreover, Tadzio and Jaschiu, were disturbingly reminiscent of Adzio and Jas, she naturally showed the book to her nephew. Adzio was amused, perhaps flattered, but, for the moment, a handsome young man leading an easy, affluent life, he was not terribly interested. In any case, he never chose to identify himself to Thomas Mann.

It was, rather, the release of Visconti's film version, sixty years later, that was for both Adzio and Jas instrumental in rekindling their interest not only in each other but in their direct personal involvement in one of the greatest works by one of the twentieth century's greatest writers. For Wladyslaw Moes's daughter, Maria Moes, now Tarchalski (who in 1971 had just arrived in Paris, in which city she has lived ever since), it was while watching *Death in Venice* alone in a minuscule Left Bank cinema that she was assailed by nostalgia for everything that she had had to leave behind her when she quit her homeland. 'I sat there and wept through it all, to the amazement and consternation of my neighbours, who found the film moving but not *that* moving.' And, almost simultaneously, between the two by then septuagenarian catalysts of the story, who had both traversed that catalogue of convulsions that we call the twentieth-century history of Poland, it prompted a first exchange of letters in many decades.

These, genuine letters written by what it is impossible not to think of as fictional characters, were haunted by the memory of the summer of 1911. Jas, who initiated the correspondence from London, where he had settled after the Second World War, had revisited the Venetian Lido two years before. Although he had found the island pretty unrecognisable, he did remark that 'I could just about place the beach where we used to build our sandcastles', adding plaintively, with reference to a squabble between their literary counterparts watched by the stricken Aschenbach, 'I swear to God I don't remember being as cruel to you as Mann describes in the book.'

Adzio hastened to reassure his old friend. 'My memory is very good,' he wrote Jas from Warsaw, 'and I still clearly remember the athletic wrestling which you always won; but the title of winner could only be gained after one's opponent was forced down on his back. So no wonder I fought till I was flat out, which obviously struck Thomas Mann as cruelty on your part.' Shades, here, as elsewhere, of Jappe and Do Escobar.

Jas shepherded his family to see the film in London's West End, but could not afford to attend its gala première, 'as the ticket prices were rather high, from 5 to 50 guineas a ticket'. (Adzio, misunderstanding a guinea to equal twenty-one pounds rather than twenty-one shillings, was aghast at how unimaginably expensive cinema seats were in England.) He, Jas, could not quite make his mind up about Visconti's adaptation. 'Undoubtedly the film is good, particularly when considered from the artistic point of view, although to my mind the plot is not very interesting and a bit difficult to follow.' There is surely something rather surreal about an individual whom we cannot help thinking of as a character in a celebrated work of fiction commenting on what he himself regards as that work of fiction's obscurities and inadequacies.

Adzio, for his part, caught the film in Paris – quite alone, as, in Maria's words, 'he would not have wanted to show his feelings about it, even to me.' He had gene-

Adzio, left, with his friend Jas in Venice, 1911

rously declined to take offence at Visconti's having neglected to pay him a visit during a lengthy talent-scouting tour of Poland in quest of *his* Tadzio (a tour about which he made a seldom-screened short film, one usually omitted from his filmography, *In Search of Tadzio*, in which the director takes an evident, malicious pleasure in showing himself in the process of inspecting bevies of schoolboys, lauding their charms with a lip-smacking 'Bellissimo! Bellissimo!').

Photo: The Kobal Collection

'Tadzio' with his friend 'Jaschiu' in Visconti's film

'It would,' he had written to Jas, 'have been detrimental [for him] to have seen an old man with all the signs of ageing when his imagination was concentrated on recreating the character of a young boy in the style of Thomas Mann.'

In reality, it was not that the Italian director was unaware of Adzio's existence. He had had some of his 'people' visit him while in Poland and had even sent him a letter apologising in advance for his intention not personally to call on him, a letter that cites exactly the same reason for the deliberately missed opportunity that Adzio himself cites in his own letter to Jas. Still, it is all a trifle baffling. While it is true that the Wladyslaw Moes of those years was in his early seventies, one would nevertheless have supposed that a director about to embark on a filmic adaptation of *Death in Venice* – or, indeed, any admirer of Mann – would have been keen to meet the person who inspired it, warts and all.

The rather delicate matter of his age apart, this 'young boy in the style of Thomas Mann' was exactly the pretty, pampered darling described in the novella. Nor did the family portrayed by Mann, albeit sketchily, differ much, at least in the superficial terms allowed by a seventy-page fiction, from that of Adzio's own.

The Moeses (that very un-Polish-sounding name is actually of Dutch origin) came from Westphalia, which had once been one of Prussia's most affluent provinces. Around the early 1830s Wladyslaw's great-grandfather, Ernest Moes, and his grandfather, Christian August, chose to resettle in Poland, where, together, they founded a prosperous textile firm in the eastern region of Bialystok. Once he was rich, and had become a pillar of the community, Christian purchased a pair of local properties, Choroszcz and Nowosiolki; then, later, in 1851, a manor house at Wierbka near Pilica, a substantially sized edifice constructed in a hybrid style, with an encrustation of turrets and ramparts, all in urgent need of renovation: it was situated near the southern city of Kielce. When renovated, this was to become the principal Moes residence, and it was there that Christian and his wife Constantia Boise raised their family, one as unusually large then as it would be now, of six sons and four daughters.

Christian August was, it seems, an extremely enlightened landowner for the period, convinced that better results were likely to be achieved with the carrot than the stick. He paid his employees decent wages and was admired in the region thereafter for having actively concerned himself with the social welfare of the workers in his factories and the peasants on his farms, building not only houses for their families but schools and even – this was really very exceptional – crèches. His particular region of Poland finding itself – as had already been, and would later so often be, the case – under Russian rule, it was by Czar Alexander II himself that a hereditary barony was eventually bestowed upon him. He died in 1872.

(Interestingly, the Wierbka house long survived

the period – from its initial purchase by the family in the nineteenth century right up to the ebbing days of the Second World War – in which it was occupied by the Moeses. It was, as we shall see, unceremoniously commandeered by the totalitarian government for the duration of the cold postwar years and later forced to earn its keep in Communist Poland as a re-education centre for drug addicts. As I write these words, however, Maria Tarchalski is in the no doubt lengthy process of taking legal action to reclaim another of her family's properties, Udorz, formerly a stud farm and equestrian centre. Even now, the question of reparation remains a vexed one, but Poland's ongoing application for membership of the European Community is likely to prove helpful to her cause.)

Adzio's father was Alexander Juliusz Moes, born in 1856; his mother, one Janina Miaczynska. After his schooling Alexander studied philosophy and chemistry in Germany, at the university of Heidelberg. It was he who inherited the property of Wierbka and what were now two paper factories both owned and managed by the Moes family, one at Wierbka, the other at Slawniow. His abiding passion was horses, a passion passed on to his son Wladyslaw – and a generation later, as it would transpire, to his grand-daughter Maria.

Family tradition has it that Alexander was as compassionately liberal a landlord and employer as his father had been before him, presiding over the local Agricultural Association and, with his wife (who would bear him two sons and four daughters), very much ahead of his time in attending to the domestic welfare of those in his employ, whether on the farm or in either of the factories. Naturally, as a fount of factual information, family tradition is often not the most objectively trustworthy of sources. Yet this perhaps partisan opinion of the man and his qualities is independently corroborated not only by the fact that he remains to this day, a century later, an esteemed figure in the region but by the even more concrete fact that in contemporary Wierbka there still exists an Alexander Moes Street.

Wladyslaw, the Adzio of our tale, was born on November 17, 1900, at Wierbka. He was the family's fourth out of six, having one elder brother, Alexander, and four sisters, Alexandra, Maria-Anna, Jadwiga and Barbara. Adzio was in fact not just born in the Wierbka manor house but like his siblings, or at least until each of them reached the age of fourteen, educated there. Instead of a single tutor, the children were accorded several apiece, each of them following his respective course of study as it was concurrently taught at the public school nearest the Moes home. They had, in addition, as members of the upper crust – Adzio's future title would be 'Baron Moes' (in Czarist Poland, as distinct from most other European countries, many male offspring, and not exclusively the eldest, inherited their father's title) – their own private French and German teachers.

The Moes children were raised in accordance with the rigorously strict guidelines in force at the time, which meant that none of them was ever permitted

Adzio in infancy

Adzio's sisters, Jadwiga, Maria-Anna
and Alexandra, with their father

to be what would be called a 'spoilt child'. Although (if their adult lives had unfolded without the unforeseen hitch of Communism) they would never have the need nor opportunity to exploit such domestic proficiencies, Adzio's sisters were taught, at a young age, cooking, sewing, ironing – all the classic 'feminine' skills – while even he was expected as a teenager to accompany his father to work in order to learn how paper was manufactured.

Maria relates her mother's brusque dismissal, when watching Visconti's film, of Silvana Mangano, the actress who played her mother-in-law, as 'not quite enough of a *grande dame*', as well as her father's incredulity when he saw Mangano not merely addressing her daughters with an unheard-of 'My dears...' but *smoking a cigarette in public*, an inadmissible liberty for a woman of her class and her period as well as a rather surprising solecism for a filmmaker who had always been famed for his obsessively finicky attention to the intricacies and idiosyncracies of *belle époque* etiquette. From the evidence of an album of Moes family photographs, some of which are reproduced in this book, Mangano actually bore no resemblance to Adzio's own mother, but was the very image of Mann's description of her fictional equivalent as tall, cool and poised, albeit with an overly narrow nose. Tantalisingly, too, from the evidence of a whole other set of photographs, there existed a disturbing physical (not to mention sartorial) kinship between the actress and the magnificently imperious Countess Carla Visconti de Modrone, the director's mother, who was very much a *grande dame*. These are perhaps deeper waters than they seem.

From the very start of his life, Adzio was singled out for special treatment. Perhaps born a little too soon after his immediately elder sister – 'My grandmother was still tired from the earlier birth,' Maria suggested to me, 'and my father was born tired' – he had a punctured lung and was in consequence a frail child. (The morbidly alert Aschenbach, noting that Tadzio's teeth are 'imperfect, rather jagged and bluish, and without a healthy glaze', conjectures with a hint of gleeful ghoulishness that 'he will most likely not live to grow old'.) So he alone of the family was allowed to sleep himself out in the morning and breakfast when it pleased him. It was, in fact, on account of that hole in his lung, and the recommendation of a Viennese specialist whom his parents had consulted that what the boy needed most was sea breezes and the company of playmates his own age, that the Moeses elected to summer in Venice (a remarkably perverse choice given the city's unsanitary reputation).

Nor, it transpires, was Thomas Mann the first writer to fall victim to his prepubescent winsomeness. At the wedding of one of his aunts – for which, as a *garçon d'honneur*, he was turned out in lace of a fetchingly creamy *blanc d'ivoire* – the six-year-old Adzio caught the eye of Henryk Sienkiewicz, the once world-famous, now world-forgotten, Nobel Prize-winning author of the much-filmed pseudo-classical romance *Quo Vadis?*. Leaving the church in his landau, the doting Sienkiewicz insisted that the infant come perch upon his knees, only hurriedly to offload him when he discovered that this Tiepolesque seraph had peed down the leg of his morning-suit.

Wladyslaw Moes, the real Tadzio

Adzio was not at all unresponsive to the privileges of beauty and, from an early age, became accustomed to being a focus of attention. During the Venetian holiday, he would strike up an acquaintance with fruit and flower vendors and inveigle them into slipping him a peach, a plum or a cluster of ripe strawberries. If they refused (which, in any event, they seldom did), he would tease them with foot-stamping squeals of 'Cattiva! Cattiva!'. Unusually, the local fishermen were permitted by his family to take him out unchaperoned on their boats. And he himself would court, as though he regarded it as no more than his rightful homage, all the petting and fondling that he came in for. He had discovered, for example, probably from his mother's precedent, the gratifying effect of delaying one's appearance in a public place; and he told Maria how eager he had been, one evening in the Hôtel des Bains, to show off to the company a pair of shiny new shoes of which he was immoderately vain. He patiently (or more likely impatiently) held back until the other guests had taken their seats. Then, with his clustering blond ringlets and water-blue eyes, he all but goose-stepped down the grand central staircase into the dining room (just like the very young Thomas Mann himself, as it happens, who would strut through the streets of his home town, Lübeck, hoping to be mistaken for the Kaiser), so intense was his resolve that no one would fail to remark on how splendidly he was shod. 'Did everyone see me?' he excitedly questioned his nurse. 'Was everyone watching?'

Someone certainly was. In his later years Adzio vividly recalled an 'old man' (Mann, remember, was thirty-six-years-old) staring at him wherever he went, hovering always just out of sight as the Moeses ambled through the city's fabled Piranesian labyrinth of tourist-worn streets and dark, sunless alleys and stairways and arches and columns and those archetypal Venetian squares whose ornamental fountains make one wonder whether the canals might have sprung a leak. He was, he recalled, at the receiving end of an especially intent gaze from his admirer when they had occasion to take the hotel lift together, an incident replicated to the last degree in both novella and film, the latter of which was widely, but perhaps unjustly, criticised for portraying a Tadzio too coquettishly self-conscious of Aschenbach's attentions. 'It's just another gentleman who likes me,' he would assure his nurse, and no one in those innocent, halcyon Edwardian days appears to have thought it worth advising him to steer altogether clear of 'old men', particularly those still in their thirties. (That, by contrast, Mann had his protagonist humiliatingly aware of the growing unease which his persistent presence was causing the grown-ups around Tadzio doubtless derived less from the facts of the case than from his own, possibly only half-articulated, stirrings of sexual culpability.)

Yet even if his mother would repeatedly tell him, 'Yes, you're good-looking, but it isn't you who have made yourself so – so there's no reason for you to be so proud of it', Wladyslaw Moes remained something of a dandy to the end of his life, no mean achievement in Communist Poland. Maria remembers him paying her a visit in Paris in 1980. 'He was then eighty years old and his life had not been an easy one. Because of inoperable cataracts, his eyesight had started to fail. But whenever we prepared to go out he would have to know that he looked just right and, as he was no longer able to check for himself, he would ask me if his shirt collar was clean and his tie straight. It was important for him to have the "look" he had always cultivated for himself.'

***

If I may permit myself a brief digression here, I think it worth posing a question that the reader, having already glanced at the photographs that illustrate this text, will probably have raised in his or her own mind: to wit, just how beautiful *was* little Wladyslaw? Beauty being, as we all know, in the eye of the beholder, each of us must come to our own individual, and inevitably subjective, conclusions. But let's consider the judgment of Tarquin Winot, the voluptuary protagonist of John Lanchester's bestselling novel *The Debt to Pleasure*, on seeing a few of these same photographs reproduced in a magazine article (written by yours truly) that he has chanced upon. 'The child in question,' Winot bitches, 'could only honestly be described as a *lump*.'

What? A lump? This infant whose facial loveliness affected Thomas Mann himself (as we now know from his intimate diaries) as much as the orchidaceous beauty of his literary facsimile affects poor, doomed Gustav von Aschenbach? A lump? This chubby-cheeked angel who stood out like a sore thumb – or, should one say, who stood out like a radiantly healthy thumb – on the beach of the Lido? A tad harsh, surely?

Yet it's perfectly true that one does experience a certain slight sense of anticlimax, a sense cruelly reinforced when photographs of the real 'Tadzio' are juxtaposed with those of his on-screen impersonator, Bjorn Andresen, the Swedish youth whom Visconti cast in his film version. So was Thomas Mann myopic? Was he blinded by love? Or was he simply wrong?

The human body never, in a sense, stands still. It is, as we learn from historical precedence, just as subject to the fickle axioms of fashion as the clothes which are designed simultaneously to conceal and reveal it. From one century to the next, from one decade to the next – these days, it feels like from one year to the next – legs have grown longer and slimmer, just as skirts have done, busts have grown more ample, blouses following suit, Rubensian carnality has gradually surrendered to Modiglianiesque angularity and Modiglianiesque angularity surrendered again to Rubensian carnality. Back and forth, forth and back, the pendulum never stops swinging.

And how this cyclical process affects us at the most elementary level is that everyone appears to get sexier in proportion as we draw closer to our own era. Human beauty, in short, not only ages but *dates*. It ages, of course, on a strictly individual level, as the bearer of such beauty finds it progressively eroded by the passage of time. But, equally, if at a far more leisurely rhythm, as modes and perceptions of physical allure unceasingly evolve, it dates on a socio-aesthetic level. The result being that someone once regarded as the absolutely unsurpassable epitome of gorgeousness gradually comes to seem, well, a lump.

It's a curious business. At any given moment, we all

have a tendency to believe that the period we ourselves live in, whichever it is, represents a kind of ideal culmination towards which the entire history of human achievement has inexorably been advancing. We simply cannot imagine what it was like to have been alive at any other time, because, for all its flaws and failures, its anxieties and absurdities, our own time *fits* us so well. Yet, eventually, this present tense of ours will be revealed as having been just as corseted in convention as any preceding it. And if what used quaintly to be called the 'vital statistics' of some current supermodel, say, impress us as having the formal *inevitability* of a geometric figure – two adjacent parallel lines for a waist, breasts on the modishly undersized side, legs so lankily long a set of rungs could be attached to them – they will sooner or later be perceived to have been just as historically determined and dateable in style as the clothes she is wearing. Even if we cannot help instinctively assuming that the continuum of feminine beauty has been ineluctably converging towards this ultimate point, her physical type, like her clothes, will end up being of interest exclusively to social historians and campy nostalgists.

And not just feminine beauty. For this evolution has, I would argue, already taken place where little

Wladyslaw Moes is concerned. So much so that it is safe to predict that the consensual cooing over Bjorn Andresen's own comeliness (when Visconti's film was released, he was dubbed 'the most beautiful boy in the world', much to the fury of the director's ex-*mignon*, Helmut Berger) will strike our descendants as hardly less inexplicable an aberration on our own generation's part as we at present regard Mann's infatuation. One day, difficult as it may be for the moment to credit, Andresen will seem just as frumpy as his turn-of-the-century model.

***

To return to 1911, the Fudakowskis, the family of Jas, who, from the evidence of period snapshots, was the more puckishly robust of the two playmates, were proprietors of a sizeable holding near the Polish-Russian frontier. The Moeses and the Fudakowskis were not, in fact, intimate friends. Yet, even if they did not travel to Venice together, nor initially put up at the same hotel, Jas's mother was acquainted with Adzio's and the families had always planned to make contact on the Lido. And, strangely, these two boys, a single brief instant of whose shared childhood was forever arrested, transfixed like a butterfly on a cork by a great writer, were thereafter to find their lives running on parallel lines. Parallel lines that were to converge, if I may employ such an oxymoron, in marriage; for, although it was only in 1988 that they met for the first time, Adzio's daughter Maria and Jas's son Wojciech are actually if very distantly related, Adzio's nephew having married the daughter of Jas's first cousin. (Readers will have to figure out the precise relationship for themselves.)

Naturally, a major upheaval in the early lives of both youths was the First World War. During the war's initial two years, continuing to pursue a vigorously nationalist military campaign against what had long been the country's traditional enemy, Russia, the Polish army, led by the eminent general and politician (and subsequent dictator) Jozef Pilsudski, fought alongside the Germans and Austrians, an allegiance which culminated in 1916 with the joint proclamation, issued by these two nations, of Poland as an independent kingdom.

The Moeses, in the south, found themselves directly in the line of fire, and the family paper mills were utterly destroyed. As for the Fudakowskis, their own estate was torched by the Russians in their attempt to stem the advance of Austrian troops. Gathering together what few belongings they could, they fled to the Ukraine, where another branch of the family lived. It was only in 1919, after the Russian Revolution, that they were able to return.

At the age of fourteen (in, therefore, the not uneventful year of 1914), Adzio had started to attend the Saint Stanislas Kostka, a small, exclusive boarding school in Warsaw, along with many of the male offspring of his parents' acquaintances; graduating four years later, he was therefore obliged to do his military service just as the war was drawing to a close. But, far from bringing relief, the armistice, too, turned out to be another traumatic event for his country. At the Treaty of Versailles, in 1919, Poland was awarded access to the Baltic Sea via what is called the Polish Corridor. Almost immediately, though, Britain's Lord Curzon drew up a border with Russia that was completely unacceptable to the Poles; and, the brand new Soviet Union having displayed, exactly as would be true again a quarter of a century later, a dogged reluctance to quit the territory which it had been illegally occupying, a second war broke out between the two enemies. And, by coincidence, both Adzio and Jas, most likely unbeknown to each other, volunteered for service in the same regiment, the First Cavalry, and both of them departed for the Russian front. (Maria remembers once being told by Adzio that her

Adzio at 16

grandmother's last words when, clasping his hand in hers, she took leave of him, were: 'You will return from this war either a living hero or a dead one.' For the Moeses there could be no third alternative.)

In that particular conflict conditions were as gruelling as would seem to be traditional to any waged on Russian soil, and the still sickly Adzio, who held the rank of sub-lieutenant, was buffeted between extremes of heat and cold, between the stifling fug of the overheated muzhiks' huts in which he would find himself billeted and the sub-zero temperatures of the rivers through which, on more than one occasion, he was forced to wade bare-chested. Yet, paradoxically, health-wise, the ordeal would turn out to be the making of him. When he was demobilised in 1921 – a peace treaty was signed at Riga to the advantage of the Poles, who, for once in the parallel history of the two nations, had defeated the Russians – the frail young man of whose literary clone Aschenbach had speculated, as we have seen, that he 'would most likely not live to grow old' had acquired an oxlike constitution which was never after to fail him, the punctured lung having seemingly healed itself in the crucible of fire and ice. He had also shown himself to be a real soldier, and returned home with a Military Cross, given for valour under fire.

As for Jas, he had been wounded in the leg during a cavalry charge against Cossack troops and, similarly awarded the Military Cross, spent several weeks recuperating in a Warsaw hospital.

The two former companions returned to a careworn land. Although a republican constitution was adopted in 1921, although some major social, agrarian and fiscal reforms were instituted, and the first faltering steps had been taken towards the country's industrialisation, Poland's was still primarily an agricultural and even feudal economy, and the condition of the peasantry remained as wretched as it had been in the nineteenth century.

Adzio, obliged by circumstances (his paralysed father, who was now approaching his seventies, was no longer capable of running the family business) to forget any ambition he might have entertained of pursuing his studies, abruptly assumed the management of the paper factories. According to his daughter, to whom he often spoke of this period as one of the hardest of his life, 'My father took very seriously the responsibility which had been forced upon him, a responsibility, to be honest, that he himself thought was a little too heavy for one of his age. Although he did not want to disappoint the family that now depended on him, he felt very much alone' – his elder brother, Alexander junior, had been allowed to continue his studies to university level – 'and, even if he wasn't devoid of either pride or ambition, he couldn't help wondering whether he possessed the strength to handle on his own all these complex business affairs for which he had never been properly prepared.'

The responsibility became even weightier when, the Moes children attaining their respective majorities within a few years of each other, the family estates were parcelled out among them. It was then, in addition to his other commitments, that Adzio became the sole proprietor of Udorz, a substantial arable farm.

Wladyslaw Moes on his farm in Poland

Young Wladyslaw Moes was evidently capable of charming the birds off the trees – he appears to have been capable, indeed, of charming the very trees themselves. Yet, although perhaps not one of nature's natural businessmen, being handsome, fond of horses, dogs and hunting, music and gaiety, fine food and wine, the designated ladies man, as it were, at many a party, ready to drop everything to set off for some ball in Warsaw or Cracow, especially during carnival season (he prided himself on his grace as a dancer), he contrived to make more than a go of the career that had been thrust upon him. No puritan but no playboy either, he somehow succeeded in mixing business with pleasure, even during the economic crisis which at the turn of the twenties and thirties affected the eastern half of Europe no less adversely than the west. Such was his life-relishing buoyancy that, at one stage in the mid-thirties, he even mooted the whimsical, never-to-be-realised, possibility of accompanying his future wife on an extended trip around the globe.

It was at a dinner hosted by mutual friends in Warsaw that Adzio first met the woman he was to marry. Anna Belina Brzozowska, the daughter of Count Wladyslaw Belina Brzozowski and Maria Rawita Ostrowska (the Ostrowskis were, and still are, one of the noblest of old Polish families), was born in the Polish capital on December 13, 1911. The Brzozowskas, like their inlaws-to-be, were of wealthy farming stock, long established in Podole, an arable region in the then Polish territory of Ukraine, a region from which they departed, either luckily or shrewdly, in order to resettle in the west, just before the outbreak of the Russo-Polish war.

The multilingual Anna (Polish apart, she was – handily, as it would turn out in later years, when times were especially gruelling – fluent in German, French and English) was educated locally in Poznan, graduated in 1923, attended a secretarial school (which was run, oddly, by nuns) in Brussels, then studied horticulture and agriculture in Switzerland before returning to Poland. She and Adzio were wed on April 27, 1935 in St Alexander's church in Warsaw. Not long after the wedding, she would offer her groom a 'Willis', a prodigiously sleek black British automobile, much-prized in prewar Poland. Although, like most of their car-owning friends, the Moeses employed a chauffeur, this was still the age of speed, the dashing, rakish and even slightly raffish Adzio was a product of that age, and he soon, capriciously, convention-defyingly, hunkered down behind the steering-wheel himself.

Throughout the thirties, then, Adzio, leading an existence as charmed and insouciant as that which he had known as an infant, would know the best of all possible worlds. A born *bon viveur*, he was acquainted with just about everyone there was to know in the modish Warsaw of the interwar years. He and Anna (who gave birth to their first child, Alexander, in 1936) were tireless party-givers and party-goers, they loved

Adzio's wedding

hunts, hunt balls and luxurious holidays in the pretty, stylish Baltic Sea resort of Jurata. His life, one crammed with events, like almost every life, but on another level fundamentally uneventful, continued thus until it would be decisively transformed in 1939.

The hapless role forced upon Poland in the warm-up to the Second World War is too familiar to need any lengthy rehearsal here. On the first day of September 1939, as everyone knows, the country was invaded, with spectacular speed and efficacy, by the Germans. It had, in effect, been betrayed by those it believed to be its allies. Earlier that year, secure from aggression (as it imagined) by promises of support from Britain and France, it had unceremoniously rejected German demands for the city of Gdansk. But when, still in 1939, Germany signed a non-aggression treaty with the Soviet Union, a treaty which included a secret clause providing for the partition of Poland between them, the country's fate was, as they say, sealed. With the Soviet army invading from the east, the Germans from the west, local resistance was swiftly crushed; and in 1941, when the Nazis attacked Russia in defiance of their pact, Poland found itself, as eventually would much of western Europe, under German occupation.

It was also in 1939 that Wladyslaw Moes was mobilised as a reserve officer and, in the last days of September, after a Polish defeat near Tomaszow Lubelski in the east of the country, taken prisoner. He was sent to a POW camp inside Germany, where he would be interned for the duration of the hostilities.

For spectators of the kind of old-fashioned war film (*The Wooden Horse*, *The Great Escape*, etc.) whose gung-ho ideology and usually upbeat action had an undeniable tendency to gloss over the Second World War's more hellish realities, the term 'POW camp'

Wladyslaw Moes in the Offlag in 1939

probably evokes no especial horrors. The camps in these films, films which were regarded by audiences of the day as 'escapist' both in a literal and figurative sense, always seemed rather jolly affairs, not so terribly different from the summer camps to which one was dispatched as a teenager, complete with cricket matches and amateur theatricals, the latter a front, of course, for some frightfully exciting and invariably successful tunnelling to freedom.

The Offlag (officers' camp) to which Adzio was sent was quite another matter. The privations were bearable at first, and the general frustration and boredom tempered not only by the camaraderie of his fellow-officers but by the various educational courses which they set about organising: Adzio, for example, taught French while studying history. But there were times in the latter years of his imprisonment, as he himself described the experience to his daughter, when, gnawed by hunger yet too proud to beg for bread from the occupants of a neighbouring German village, he would stretch out on his bunk, enlace his fingers over his chest and, almost willing himself to die – *dying to die*, as it were – prepare himself for what he was convinced was the end.

It wasn't. His life was saved *in extremis* by the delayed but, because of that delay, all the more welcome arrival of packages flown in by the International Red Cross. At last, in 1945, shaken but not broken, half-starved but alive, he was liberated by the British. And it was for the British that he remained on active military duty for a further year on German soil, as an interpreter and liaison officer.

In the Communist Poland of the war's immediate aftermath, however, what he was to discover was that, like many of his former set, he had lost everything. Absolutely everything – from the family's houses, properties and paper mills down to its furniture, its jewellery and even its clothes – had been confiscated by the state. As his entire life attests, Adzio possessed the resilience indispensable to all survivors, but he would have been less than human had he not felt bitterness at the treatment he received, a bitterness intensified by the fact that, as was demonstrated by the street named after his father, the Moes family had always taken pride in its benign, forward-looking influence over the social welfare of the workers, farmers and peasants on its estates. One of Adzio's own sisters, Jadwiga, had, indeed, died of tuberculous contracted during the period when she ministered to the families of their employees, while another, the youngest, Barbara, was left with a single lung. As Maria Tarchalski told me, 'It's true that my father enjoyed the privileges of his title, but he also believed that he and his whole family had worked hard and benevolently and hadn't deserved to be stripped of their social and professional rank.'

He was, of course, not alone in having been punished for having been born to a life of privilege. During the closing months of the war, while he was still languishing in his POW camp, his wife, solely on account of her aristocratic lineage, had spent two months in a Polish prison, where, incongruously, she met up with all her former acquaintances, the whole chic clique that had been frequented by the Moeses in the thirties. Anna, who was later to be reunited with her little nine-year-old son Alexander in Cracow, was ever after haunted and harrowed by terrifying recollections of the interrogation rooms and torture chambers which she had been ordered to mop up.

Although Adzio initially had no intention of settling again in a Poland by whose government he knew he would be treated, by definition, as a parasite and pariah, the problem, one that had to be confronted by a number of his fellow ex-POWS, was that his family was trapped. Anna and her son had already been ejected from the family's home by the Communist government, which allowed her to leave with no more than a single small suitcase. Whatever could not be packed into that small suitcase had to be abandoned. Yet, even in those dire days, not quite everything was lost. A handful of her jewels, which she had left concealed about the house, were missed by its ruthless ransackers after their departure and subsequently recuperated; and if Maria still possesses her mother's engagement ring, it is because one of her mother's maids had squirrelled it away and returned it to her when it was politic to do so.

A plot was hatched by Adzio to engineer the escape of Anna and Alexander; Maria no longer knows why it failed, only that it did. Her father, in consequence, finally had to re-enter Poland in 1946, with just a few coins in his pocket. It was his homeland, but it was also a land from which he had been exiled for almost seven years. It was a land, moreover, in which he realised all too well that there would be no place for him or his like.

Deciding, nevertheless, to make the best of the situation, he and Anna moved to Jelenia Gora in the south-west of the country, which is where his daughter Maria was born the following year. And it was at that period that, ill-equipped for the drab rigours of the postwar world, Wladyslaw Moes began to drift through a long and disheartening series of more or less menial occupations while at the same time striving to hold his family together. Such a precipitous and, as he felt, unwarranted demotion in his social status did engender the resentment one would expect, although it was cushioned by the fact that all their fashionable prewar friends were suddenly finding themselves in the same boat.

In view of the modest salaries they were likely to earn, husband and wife were both forced to go to work. Anna was employed as a secretary, while Adzio, no doubt because of his prewar career, got a job in a local paper factory (one which, as Maria acidly remarks, 'had certainly been stolen from someone else'). In fact, he was, in all but name, manager of that factory, just as he had been of his own in the interwar years. Yet, being of the *gratin* still, and hence *persona non grata*, his official ranking in the hierarchic structure of the state-controlled business was that of unskilled labourer, with a wage-packet to match.

Ironically, it was his success at running the factory which prompted his abrupt departure from it. In 1947 he was offered the chance of a better position, and by extension a better salary, if he would agree to become a member of the Party. He refused, and was instantly dismissed. Indeed, to the end of his days, although he was eventually able to contemplate the past, both his own and his country's, without the sepia-tinted glasses of nostalgia, he remained a ferocious anti-Communist and was never once heard to acknowledge the existence, in the Marxist cloud that hung over Poland, of even the most attenuated of silver linings. Maria remembers how distressed she was as an adolescent, when she had landed a leading role in her school's end-of-term play, to discover that her father refused to attend the performance, since he could not countenance meeting the headmaster, who was, probably by obligation, even coercion, rather than out of any genuine ideological conviction, a Party member. Even if she understood why it had to be so, she found it difficult to forgive his absence.

Having lost the only job for which he was really trained, Adzio accepted an erratic variety of employments. He first worked as a bookkeeper for an import-export company in Warsaw, while Anna became a secretary in a state-owned publishing house. The family – which consisted now of the couple itself, their son Alexander and recently born daughter Maria – lived in modest rented accommodation out in one of the capital's suburbs, Komorow. 'The situation,' says Maria, 'was difficult and the atmosphere extremely unpleasant.' The Moeses could not help but be aware that they continued to be the object of heavy bureaucratic suspicion, aware that they were permanently under surveillance, on practically a day-to-day basis, perceptible, reminisces Maria, even to the child that she was. The harassment – the summary interrogations, the repeated, pointless examination of their papers – finally led to Adzio losing this job as he had his previous one and having to accept a post in Komorow itself as foreman on a construction site.

By the early fifties, however, the hardships began to ease up for him as for the rest of the country. The once wealthy Moeses had managed to put by a few savings and, with the assistance of Adzio's elder sister Alexandra (who had meanwhile migrated to the United States) and the two others who were still alive (both of whom lived in Poland), they bought a small bungalow in 1954 which they succeeded in furnishing with those rare items of furniture from Wierbka that had been salvaged from the débâcle.

From that point on, they enjoyed a greater degree of material comfort, although there were still difficult times ahead. One telling confirmation of Adzio's reduced circumstances is the fact that when, in the seventies, he saw Visconti's *Death in Venice*, and was amazed to hear his own family name 'Moes', which nowhere figures in Mann's novella, pronounced perfectly audibly on the soundtrack (in the scene in which a distraught Aschenbach enquires of the hotel

Wladyslaw Moes and son Alexander, an Adzio lookalike

receptionist whose luggage it is that he sees waiting
to be loaded on to a vaporetto), he mused aloud in
one of his letters to Jas whether he ought to consult a
lawyer on the matter of potential compensation. And,
indeed, given Visconti's reluctance, when he toured
Poland, to obtain Wladyslaw Moes's personal blessing
on the project, the inclusion of his name in the film, a

Adzio at the same age as Alexander

quite meaningless in-joke for the ordinary spectator, does strike one as a gratuitous intrusion into the man's privacy.

In December 1955 the Moeses suffered a tragedy more painful than any they had ever known, the death from leukemia of their son Alexander, who was by then a strapping nineteen-year-old apparently bursting with good health and mad on sports. This, in the words of Maria, was just too much to bear. 'My parents were devastated. I have memories of my mother permanently in tears.' One day, not long after Alexander's funeral, while they were all having lunch together, they happened to hear Chopin's 'Marche funèbre' on the radio. 'Both of my parents, who had always been too proud to externalise their sufferings, broke down in front of me. I've never forgotten it. And, from that day forward, we never again listened to a note of Chopin's music.'

Life, though, did go on. If they didn't listen to Chopin, they listened to opera and operetta, to the latest records of Sinatra, Maurice Chevalier and Yves Montand. They appeared to have been rather a francophile family altogether. Maria remembers how, as a teenager, she would look forward to the weekly arrival in the household of the latest number of the French photo-journalistic magazine *Paris-Match*. And, whatever were the family's budgetary difficulties, Adzio declined to penny-pinch on food and wine. Says Maria, 'At table he would always insist on having a bottle of Chablis, even his favourite, Châteauneuf-du-Pape.' She recalls too how, after her mother had found new employment as a secretary in the Greek Embassy in Warsaw, and her father similar employment as a relatively well-paid interpreter in the Iranian Embassy (where most of the business seems to have been conducted in French), Adzio began once more, as he had in his twenties, to fuss over his appearance. 'He had a large, elegant wardrobe of hand-made suits, shirts, jackets and ties – the latter, although smart, always extremely classic and sober. He would never be seen in public not wearing a suit and hat. It wasn't easy being well-dressed in the Poland of the fifties, but he somehow carried it off.'

Yet, so entrenched was the institutional paranoia, even in those fairly relaxed years a family like the Moeses was not to be left alone. It would sometimes happen, for example, that because both husband and wife worked in foreign embassies, albeit in far from senior capacities, diplomats would meet at their home. (Adzio was, after all, a baron, even if, because all such Czarist-conferred titles were no longer recognised by the state, he was now officially at the bottom of the social, and socialist, heap.) On these occasions the surveillance of the Moeses' humdrum comings and goings, which had never completely lapsed, would suddenly intensify. As long as their acquaintances among the diplomatic community were being entertained by them within, automobiles whose very anonymity identified them as police cars would warily circle the little bungalow in the Warsaw suburb. Wladyslaw Moes himself was more than once invited by the secret police to act as a spy inside the embassy where he was employed.

Since none of this harassment had borne fruit, the secret police coming to the realisation, after so many years, that it was a waste of time, money and resources, it was finally phased out. Yet old habits die hard. When Visconti's *Death in Venice* opened in 1971, and not merely Adzio but the world (that part of the world, at least, that could possibly be interested) heard the name of 'Moes' pronounced by the receptionist of the Hôtel des Bains, a group of German journalists made their way to Komorow in order to interview the original Tadzio. Then again, doubtless dreading some indiscretion from the 'former' baron Moes, the ex-landowning aristocrat to whom Communism was known to be anathema, police cars were nervously staked out in front of the house.

For the most part, however, the Moeses had access during these years to the same limited freedoms as any other Poles. They began once more, as they had in better days, to vacation on the Baltic Sea and spent weekends visiting friends in Cracow, putting up at decent if hardly palatial hotels, or else toured the lakelands at Mazury in the northeast of Poland. The

Wladyslaw Moes with capercaillies

two spots which Adzio categorically refused to visit were the family's former properties in Udorz and Wierbka. Such distressing excursions would, in any case, have had to be undertaken clandestinely, as former landowners were prohibited by law from re-visiting what had once been their estates.

Maria, on the other hand, did secretly make the trip out to the manor house of which she had heard so much but in which she had never lived. Later in 1971, when, with a group of friends (one of whom she married), she decided to defect, she received, after two initial rejections, a passport for what was ostensibly to be a ten-day holiday in Vienna, but only on condition that her father deposit a cheque with the Polish treasury which would, in the event of her failing to return to Poland, reimburse the state for the entire five-year term of her studies at the Warsaw Polytechnic, then drawing to an end. This Wladyslaw Moes did. From Vienna, Maria and her friends travelled on to Paris, where she and her husband-to-be, who was also an engineering student, elected to remain rather than beginning a new life in Canada or South Africa as they had originally planned.

That lost deposit represented a substantial sum for Adzio, but he could see no future for Maria in a Communist Poland. The real sacrifice was, of course, the departure of his daughter, one made all the more severe by the fact that the Moeses had already lost their son. Yet even if it must have occurred to parents and daughter alike that they might not see each other again, Maria recalls a curiously unemotional parting scene – rather as when Adzio had gone to war – her father and mother resolved to preserve their arist-ocratic sang-froid to the end.

After Anna's death in 1978 (she had been ailing for several years), and the progressive relaxation of travel restrictions in Poland – a sadistic ruling in the country allowed elderly citizens, who were regarded as unlikely potential defectors, to go abroad, although always alone, never in the company of a husband or wife – the francophile Adzio would more than once journey to Paris to spend time with his daughter. It was on one of these trips that he broke his femur, an accident which left him mildly incapacitated for the remainder of his days. And what seriously worsened an already awkward situation, given his advanced age, was the blood transfusion he was given in a Parisian hospital: the blood was contaminated. He contracted viral hepatitis, a disease from which he never fully recovered; and no longer capable, now in his eighties, of looking after himself, he started to share life in his suburban house with one of his cousins, an unmarried woman.

Wladyslaw Moes died in Warsaw, at the age of 86, on December 17 1986. His daughter Maria, afraid not only for herself, for her freedom to return to Paris, but for her own daughter, with whom she was pregnant, did not attend the funeral.

A few years before his death, however, an event had occurred that makes one wonder whether some lives are not palindromes, readable in both directions at once. Like his former companion Jas before him, and perhaps for much the same reason, Adzio decided that he would like, just once, to revisit Venice. But the trip had to be called off at the last minute. He was to be turned away from the city, in a freakish coincidence, because of a cholera scare.

Adzio at the end of his life

***

There was to be another curious incident at the end of Adzio's life – the moment when, after so many years, he and Jas once more came face to face. Even more curiously, the setting for their eleventh-hour reunion was neither Warsaw nor Venice but a large house near Wimbledon Common. It might, then, be useful to open a brief flashback here to find out what has been happening to Adzio's former companion, whom we left recuperating in hospital from a leg wound received in the Bolshevik-Polish war of 1920.

Unlike his childhood chum, Jan Fudakowski did attend university, where he studied agricultural engineering. But his father, inconsolable at the destruction of his estate and, moreover, one of the millions of victims of the virulent influenza epidemic which swept Europe in the war's immediate wake, chose to sell his property outright (to the Wielowieyski family, a name which oddly figures in the Moes family tree) for what must have seemed like a goodly sum of money at the time but whose value, less than three months later, had been decimated by the stratospherically high inflation which was to destroy the nation's economy. Jas married in the twenties and bought another and more modest farm which, though, chanced to be located smack on the second line of defence against East Prussia. The Fudakowskis were thus among the first to be evacuated in 1939.

Jas was immediately mobilised and, on the military defeat and occupation of Poland, interned in Lithuania. He escaped from his internment camp, making his way to Sweden, then to France, where the Polish free forces were billeted. Evacuated out from Perpignan in 1940, he rejoined the 10th Polish Mounted Rifles, a tank regiment, in Scotland. Later he was assigned by the Polish Government-In-Exile, which was based in London, to its Ministry of Agriculture; and, after the war ended, he joined UNRRA (whose initials stand for the 'United Nations Relief and Rehabilitation Association') in Vienna, where the family was reunited. Wojciech, his son, who was now himself of an age for military service, met up with the rest of his kinfolk in Austria by the elementary expedient of quitting Poland as though he were setting off on leave and never returning. Later still, the Fudakowskis decamped to London and eventually – and, as it would turn out, permanently – settled in England.

What lay ahead for Jan Fudakowski were hard, albeit not embittered, times. His son remembers him as 'a self-sacrificing man who was never afraid of facing up to real hardship for our sakes. He remained optimistic, and he lived forward not backward. To be a Pole in the twentieth century you have to learn to be adaptable.'

In England he could no longer practise his own profession and had to accept whatever jobs were offered him. Most interesting, at least *pour la petite anecdote*, was that of administrator of Harlaxton Manor in Lincolnshire, which had been adapted as a college for Jesuits. The house was located near Grantham, practically next door to that grocer's shop and the flat above it in which the town's now most notorious resident, Margaret Thatcher, was conceived: from *Death in Venice* to 'Life in Downing Street' is one of those cultural shortcuts, or short-circuits, which only history, not fiction, is willing to effect. (It would be pleasant to be able to add that Wojciech, who specialised in the same field, industrial chemistry, as Thatcher, studied alongside her, but even history has shied from tying up that particular knot in our narrative.)

Jas found life as an émigré no sinecure. The charming Metrolandish house in Wimbledon in which he lived to the end of his days, and whose archtypal British exterior contrasted with the evocative

Polish memorabilia with which its rooms were filled, was purchased not by him but for him by his children. And it was there, in 1973, that Adzio, paying a brief visit to England, was taken by his nephew, who lived in Ealing. Although their children no longer recall with any assurance when they had last met, it had undoubtedly been prior to the Second World War.

Alas, we shall never know what they might have had to say to one another, these two men who were older now by far than Thomas Mann when he first sighted them frolicking together on the beach of the Lido; older, too, much older, than Gustav von Aschenbach when he was rowed across the Stygian lagoon – by a sullen, incommunicative Charon perched on the stern of his gondola as though walking the tightrope on the water – to meet his death in Venice.

***

Adzio has, of course, been survived by Tadzio, his literary twin. His own existence has been obliterated by that of Mann's half-factual, half-fictional creation, who was destined to become one of the most vivid and powerful cultural icons of the twentieth century (and beyond), almost as easily identifiable to those who have never read *Death in Venice* as to those who have.

How, and why, did such a process of mythification –
and also, as we have seen, of mystification – occur?

That it has occurred over the past nine decades is
irrefutable, even if, for the moment, we discount the
single work, not excluding Mann's original novella,
which has been most responsible for propagating and
perpetuating the Tadzio myth, Visconti's cinematic
adaptation.

Of that film, more later. Its influence may be
measured, however, by the probable truth that it was
less Mann's than Visconti's *Death in Venice* which
prompted Benjamin Britten to write his operatic
version, although the prior existence of the film was
also the cause of a protracted copyright dispute over
whose long-delayed resolution Britten despaired. In
fact, encouraged by Golo Mann, Thomas's youngest
son (who also informed him that his father had
thought him the ideal composer for an opera of his
novel *Dr Faustus*), Britten had begun to collaborate
with his librettist, the painter John Piper, even before
the rights to the novella had been secured.

The opera was premiered at the Aldeburgh Festival
in June 1973. The tenor Peter Pears, the composer's
vocal Muse and personal companion, sang the leading
part of Aschenbach; the baritone John Shirley-Quirk
incarnated a multiplicity of roles: the goatish old

fop encountered on the ferry, the truculent gondolier, the hotel manager, the fusspot of a barber who
sets himself the unenviable challenge of 'prettifying'
Aschenbach for the climactic scene, and so on; and
Tadzio (an inappropriately muscly youth in the
original production) was not sung at all but danced.
The opera has since found a respectable niche in the
international repertoire, although it is fair to say that,
maybe because of the innate resistance of the source
material to theatrical staging, it is not, nor is it ever
likely to be, among the most highly or warmly regarded of Britten's compositions.

He himself remained ever after in two minds about
the work's value. To Frederick Ashton, who choreo-
graphed Tadzio's dances on the beach of the Lido, he
remarked that its score was 'either the best or the
worst music I've ever written' – frankly, it's neither one
nor the other – adding, enigmatically and teasingly,
that he had 'a terrible dread of playing the piece
to anyone'. But it was to the younger composer Colin
Matthews that he came closest to showing his hand,
perhaps even revealing the degree to which he had
come to identify with Aschenbach. When, on reading,
in an article in *Opera* magazine, that the subject of
Death in Venice, as of all his works for the stage,
was 'loss of innocence', he hurled the magazine out of

his sight with a furious 'That's absolute rubbish!'

Matthews diplomatically kept his own counsel in Britten's presence, but did admit to wondering what other subject could conceivably be attributed to them. And, in reality, the theme of the disturbing impact that young male beauty may have on an individual who himself is neither young nor beautiful was not new to the composer. In 1951 he had already adapted for the operatic stage, adapted more effectively than *Death in Venice*, what is still arguably the most celebrated of all such fictions, Herman Melville's *Billy Budd*.

Visconti and Britten have been the two most prominent adaptors of Mann's novella. Yet, considering the insatiable vampirism of contemporary cultural forms, the indecent relish with which a medium, a genre, even an individual text, will feast off another without so much as a by-your-leave, it tends to be the case that the mythic status of any work of art is more accurately to be gauged by the frequency of references made to it in the *interstices* of a culture, on its margins rather than in its mainstream. It is, then, less by the existence of Visconti's film or Britten's opera that we are alerted to *Death in Venice*'s iconic resonance than by a cluster of more peripheral, occasionally uncaptioned, appropriations of its textures and trappings.

These range from a colour-supplement profile in the *Sunday Times*, dating from the early seventies, of François-Marie Banier, Paris's erstwhile 'Golden Boy', whose five-page spread included a photograph of the sultry young author in a Tadziesque sailor-suit, to the fleetingly glimpsed appearance, during the Venetian climax of Paul Mazursky's 1973 film comedy *Blume in Love*, of an anachronistic Aschenbach and Tadzio strolling arm in arm among the tourists and pigeons on the Piazza San Marco. Or from a tiny volume, *Le Malheur au Lido*, a delightful parody of Mann written in 1987 by the French poet and novelist Louis-René des Forêts as a homage to his friend and fellow-writer Pierre Klossowski – the 'Malheur' of the title, a title that might be translated as 'The Unfortunate Incident on the Lido', is naturally a pun on the name 'Mahler', just one sign of how Visconti's film, with its indelible soundtrack score, had already usurped the prestige of Mann's text – to Harold Brodkey's novel *Profane Friendship*, a homoerotic romance that would not have been possible without Mann's prior example. Or from the impersonation of Tadzio (sailor-suited again) by Peter Schlesinger, David Hockney's boyfriend, in Jack Hazan's film *A Bigger Splash* to a kitschy, ludicrously ill-judged stage version of the novella by the Citizens Theatre of Glasgow.

photo: Eve Arnold/Magnum Photos

François-Marie Banier

There was, finally (if I may introduce a personal note here), a novella of my own, later filmed, *Love and Death on Long Island*, which reinvented Mann's tale as the account of a lonely, elderly English writer's thralldom to the pulpy glamour of an American teen idol. In that novella I, too, like des Forêts, and in the same fashion, exposed rather than tried to conceal my debt to Mann. The title, for example, which I had my protagonist give his novel-in-progress was *Adagio*, a punning allusion not just to the adagio (more pre-cisely, adagietto) of Mahler's Fifth Symphony but equally to the name 'Tadzio' itself or, as Aschenbach mishears it, 'Adgio'. (Just for the record, I also once wrote a short story, published in a French collection, about a visitor to a museum, one in which a Canaletto retrospective is being held, who furtively stalks an adolescent boy past one Venetian landscape after another.)

Visconti's film now. It was first screened at the 1971 Cannes Festival, where, to the director's teeth-gnashing chagrin, it failed to win the Palme d'Or, which was awarded instead to Joseph Losey's and Harold Pinter's *The Go-Between*. (Visconti, who abruptly returned to Italy in a very public huff, was slightly mollified when the film was selected later in the same year for the Royal Command Performance in London.) Writing in 1976 to a journalist, Gilles Jacob, who would later become director of the Cannes Festival himself, François Truffaut claimed that the jury had decided to *punish* the director – *punish* was not merely his word but his emphasis – for having, as he put it, 'taken the prize for granted'. He then went on to offer a very credible argument for the lasting popularity of the film, especially if compared to the now pretty much forgotten *Go-Between*:

Death in Venice is endlessly screened in art cinemas because, in formal terms, it's an almost perfect film and one which has stood up well over the years; partly because of Mahler, but also because of a unity of tone in style and subject-matter, people like the film the way they like a record and they go and see it again and again.

Truffaut is right. Visconti was an infinitely more enigmatic artist than he strikes one at first glance. Marshalling scores of extras, zooming into one glittering *objet d'art* after another, positively wallowing in acres of ormolu and crystal, he seemed to make his opulent period films in exactly the same way that television directors make their plushly upholstered classic serials. Yet his are masterly and theirs aren't. Why? *Mystère*, as the French say, particularly as he, too, was unintimidated by classic texts. (He also adapted Boîto, Verga, Dostoevsky, Lampedusa and d'Annunzio.) In fact, Visconti was the supreme, and arguably even the sole, exception to the rule that, in the cinema, the better the work adapted, the worse is likely to be the adaptation. Precisely why, though, did he choose to film *Death in Venice*?

Demanding of a critic that he or she discourse on Visconti's career without once employing the term 'contradiction' would be akin to forcing someone to define a spiral staircase with both hands tied behind his back. The Marxist prince, the nineteenth-century-ish aesthete who became one of the giants of the twentieth century's quintessential art form, the director whose films were repeatedly described as 'operatic' just as his opera stagings tended to be called 'cinematic' – these have long been the staples, the clichés, of Viscontian exegesis. Clichés, naturally, are to be avoided; yet this particular set has proved especially tenacious.

But are they true? As with most clichés, the answer is yes and no. Yes, Visconti was indeed a prince, his surname practically a generic signifier of aristocratic lineage; more debatable is the question of whether he was ever anything but a drawing-room Marxist. And, yes, he was drawn as an adaptor to the work of the mostly nineteenth-century literary geniuses mentioned above. Yet it is equally the case that, adaptations and original screenplays alike, the majority of his films were set in the present day. As for the opera/cinema dialectic, there is nothing remotely operatic (by which, in this context, is meant hieratic and stagy) about such masterpieces as *Ossessione*, *White Nights* and even *The Leopard*.

From a loftier overview, moreover, these outwardly

oxymoronic labels can actually be shown to have been mutually compatible. As a young man dazzled by the political and intellectual effervescence of interwar Paris, the city in which he was based during the Popular Front, it was all but inevitable that he would be influenced by the vigorous promotion of a common cause between avant-gardist art and socialist politics in which most of the French intelligentsia were united. All but inevitable, too, that he would launch his career in the cinema with two of the key works of neo-realism, *Ossessione* (an unacknowledged and unpaid-for version of James M. Cain's *The Postman Always Rings Twice*) and *La Terra Trema*, a drama about the exploitation of poor Sicilian fishermen, adapted from a novel by the master of *verismo*, Giovanni Verga.

Yet, paradoxically, this Visconti was not at all inconsistent with the filmmaker of *Death in Venice*. Like many a middle- and upper-class fellow traveller, what fascinated him in Marx's theories of the historical process was less the class struggle as such, less the economic salvation of the oppressed proletariat, than the concomitant decline and (as was believed at the time) eventual eradication of the dominant caste to which he himself belonged. Like the kind of dilettante whose decision to 'go over to Rome' derives more from bewitchment with the liturgical trappings of the

Catholic Church than from any revealed faith in its doctrines, Visconti was less attracted to the necessarily austere iconography of the working classes than to that, with its instant aesthetic appeal, of the foredoomed *ancien régime*. He may have affected to talk of *Death in Venice* as 'not decadent or aesthetic or hedonistic, but, more seriously and in a manner that is basically Greek, [as a quest] for perfection, for total harmony', but he was patently less galvanised, here as elsewhere in his work, by dreams of a classless society than aroused, and it would not be going too far to suggest that he was erotically aroused, by the deliciously suppurating spectacle of what he expected would be the bourgeoisie's irreversible decay.

Naturally, it's impossible to know what was going on inside his head, but the above would seem to be a reasonable reading of his anomalous status as a film-maker. And it does help to explain why so seemingly apolitical a film as *Death in Venice* really cannot be written off, as several commentators have done, as an uncritical wallow in passéist upper-class nostalgia. Visconti was far too lucid an artist to remain insensitive to the ideological tensions which underlay even the most apparently superficial of his works and too cunning a manipulator of filmic narrative not to know how to turn them to his advantage.

If Mann's *Death in Venice* constituted, as I shall endeavour to show, both the apotheosis and critique of a socio-sexual tradition, then Visconti's, while being also that, represented, to anyone wishing to get more

Photo: The Kobal Collection

Luchino Visconti directing Bjorn Andresen

out of his films than just ecstatic appreciation of the stylishness of their furniture and fittings (not excluding what might be called their human furnishings and fittings), the postmortem of a culture.

Where Truffaut errs, however, is in his proposal that *Death in Venice* is some kind of a perfect film. It is much too slavishly imitative for that, resembling a chip off the True Cross (and scarcely more authentic than most such chips are). It is hobbled, moreover, by a slew of redundant expositional scenes – notably, the horribly stilted debates, on the crowning point and purpose of artistic creation, between Aschenbach and a fellow-composer, purportedly based on Schoenberg, just as Aschenbach himself was based on Mahler. (In the novella Aschenbach is a writer, in the film a composer, but the conceit of 'disguising' Dirk Bogarde as Mahler cannot be regarded as a betrayal of Mann on Visconti's part, since Mann's own description of Aschenbach's physical appearance, as also his choice of Mahler's first name, Gustav, for that of his protagonist, clearly invites the reader to make the same connection.) But it is, nonetheless, as Truffaut implies by comparing it to a record, and hence to music, an insidiously memorable one. There is a hypnotic quality to the passages (the 'hymnic passages', as Mann referred to the corresponding pages of his novella) in which the besotted Aschenbach is portrayed what one can only describe as 'cruising' Tadzio. And even if Visconti's reconstruction of the moeurs and manners of the turn-of-the-century *beau monde* was, as we have seen, a shade less flawless than might have been expected from his reputation as a maestro of historical detail, what he offered was, if not perfection, then at least a persuasive illusion of perfection. So much so, it is extremely difficult to imagine someone reading the novella after watching the film and mentally visualising both its characters and locations independently of and thus differently from the director's own vision.

The ultimate test of the film's credibility is, of course, Tadzio himself. And there it can be said that, if Visconti's Aschenbach, because patently not Mann's, will be by extension not everyone's (although this ought not to be construed as a criticism of the admirable and sometimes brilliant Bogarde), Bjorn Andresen has become, once and for all time, the Tadzio of the collective imagination. Indeed, I would be prepared to claim, *pace* Truffaut, that the real key to the film's popularity is the fact that Visconti discovered for the role of Tadzio an adolescent so ravishing that for once spectators, including readers of Mann, had the impression of justice having been done to a reputedly matchless model. Mann himself spoke of the circumstances of *Death in Venice*'s gestation as a species of miracle. The miracle of Visconti's film version was the casting of Andresen. Had he been less beautiful, the film would have been less good. It really is as elementary as that. (If one not wholly credible account is to be believed, Visconti's producers were so terrified that the film would be seen as solely for a gay audience they tentatively proposed that the part of Tadzio be rewritten for a young girl!)

It's not impossible, however, that, like Mann six decades before him, Visconti started to feel some obscure stirrings of dissatisfaction with his film, not impossible that he was troubled, again like Mann, by its 'errors and weaknesses', its 'half-baked ideas and falsehoods'. All of which is, to be sure, little more than speculation, except that, unlike Mann, Visconti did contrive to make *Death in Venice* over again. In 1973, a mere two years after its release, he shot what was perhaps the most personal, the most (obliquely) auto-biographical film of his entire career, a film which, significantly, shared an identical narrative premise with *Death in Venice*. This was *Conversation Piece* – its Italian title is *Gruppo di Famiglia in un Interno*, which means the same thing, and its uncharac-teristically gross French title is *Violence et Passion*, which of course does not – and it starred Burt Lancaster, Helmut Berger and Silvana Mangano, the same actress who had played Tadzio's mother.

A brief recap of its plotline will immediately point up its affinity with *Death in Venice*, even though, on this occasion, the action of the film takes place in Rome and almost exclusively inside the protagonist's apartment. Lancaster plays an elderly professor, a collector of paintings, specifically eighteenth-century 'conversation pieces', permanently reminded of his divorced and childless condition by the painted families of others which surround him in his sealed and padded environment. One day, out of the blue, his cloistered intimacy is perturbed by the eruption into his life of a group of drug-addicted, neo-Fascistic students – in particular, by the torridly charismatic young Konrad (Berger), with whom he haplessly falls in love. The theme of the film is therefore, yet again, that of the intellectual teased and finally torn out of his carapace by an unworthy object of desire.

This time, however, whatever were the director's own protestations – 'He is egocentric,' Visconti said of his protagonist to one interviewer, 'a man shut in on himself who, instead of forming relationships with other people, collects pictures of them. I'm not that egotistical. I have so many friends' – it is irresistibly tempting to interpret the principal character as a self-portrait, especially as the actor whom he cast as his surrogate's passion was his own former lover. Lancaster, at least, seems to have had no doubts as to the real identity of his character and, without any argument from the director, got a handle on the role by mimicking Visconti's gestural tics and attitudes.

Since Visconti's death *Conversation Piece* has become something of a cult movie. Certainly, for those who regarded *Death in Venice* as, to quote one scurrilous French critic, 'a fantasy for masturbators who prefer to keep their trousers on', a pusillanimous film whose princely director exploited his *droit de seigneur* over both a masterpiece of literature (Mann's novella) and a masterpiece of nature (the young Bjorn Andresen), without risking any greater investment of self than the vainglorious flaunting of his own unimpeachably tasteful concupiscence and culture, it was the latter work which, for all its obvious flaws, was the true 'adaptation' of Mann's novella. It was, if nothing else, a brave, sometimes even embarrassingly brave, attempt to draw up to the surface everything which had always been repressed not merely in Visconti's cinema – a cinema which constantly flirted, yet did no more than flirt, with homosexuality – but in Mann's fiction.

Finally, before we leave the film version of *Death In Venice*, it might be worth asking what happened, following its international release, to Bjorn Andresen, the 'third' Tadzio.

For any spectator of the short *In Search of Tadzio* there is instantly no doubt at all, when Andresen bashfully steps forward in the classroom of a Swedish high school to be given the once-over by the lynx-eyed director, that the quest is over. But, even before he was selected by Visconti, the fifteen-year-old's life had been incident-packed. He was born in 1955, out of wedlock, and was never thereafter to learn the identity of his father, although a persistent rumour had it that he was a prominent member of the Swedish Academy, the organisation which awards Nobel Prizes (one of which was, of course, won by Thomas Mann in 1929). In the year of Andresen's birth, his mother married a Norwegian businessman – hence the name Bjorn – whom she divorced only four years after. Then, in 1965, just five years before his encounter with Visconti, she disappeared and was later discovered to have committed suicide. Bjorn was raised by his grandparents.

The film, as we know, went around the world and its 'godlike beauty' of a hero, as one critic baptized him, followed it, without ever really enjoying the experience of frantic young girls ripping off his clothes at premieres in London, Berlin and Tokyo. But his entire career, if that word truly can be applied to a wretched ragbag of appearances in now forgotten films (*Swedish Love Story? Bluff Stop?*), was calamitously mismanaged by his agent. For the role in *Death in Venice* itself, for example, he was paid precisely five thousand dollars, which had impressed him as an outlandish amount of money (and with which he at once bought an electric piano), until Dirk Bogarde casually let slip that he had received a hundred times as much. In his later years, as a classically trained musician who had once had adolescent aspirations of founding a rock band, he was responsible for the musical arrangements of a Swedish stage production of *The Rocky Horror Show* and he himself played John Lennon in a short-lived show about the Beatles. But nothing worked for him, and he had become a virtual has-been by his early twenties.

Nor did he have much luck in his private life. Like Adzio, Tadzio lost one of his children. An apparently happy marriage broke up after only a few years because of the cot death, at nine months, of his second, a son.

When last heard of (which was, to be sure, a long time ago), his personal circumstances had apparently got back on track and he had been reunited with his estranged wife and daughter. As for his professional life – well, perhaps in Sweden they still remember him. Yet the truth would appear to be that his face was as much his misfortune as his fortune. To a British journalist, who interviewed him when he was in his twenties, he said, 'I can't wait to age. I was born with a face I did not ask for.' Then he added (and although the sentiments expressed are scarcely original, and the high-falutin turn of phrase suggests that the statement was, in any event, cobbled together by the journalist in question, it's still perhaps relevant to a book about the Tadzio myth): 'One of the diseases of the world is that we associate beauty with youth. We are wrong. The eyes and the face are the windows of the soul and these become more beautiful with the age and pain that life brings. True ugliness comes only from having a black heart.'

***

In 1929, as I wrote above, Mann was awarded at last the Nobel Prize which he already craved in 1911 and *Death in Venice* increasingly became, among much else, the paradigmatic master-text of homosexual eroticism. It's true that the form of desire depicted by Mann was both closeted and ultimately frustrated, a fact which seems to make Aschenbach, on the face of it, an uncongenial role model for the modern type of uncomplicated gay man who is, as the French phrase it, comfortable in his skin. Partly, however, because of *Death in Venice*'s perfection as a literary artefact, partly because no fiction of comparable quality, novel or novella, 'positive' or not, has since succeeded in dislodging it from the Pantheon, and partly because the unrequited passion of an older for a younger man – although one seldom as young as Mann's Tadzio – remains even now, if everyone is honest about it, a dispiriting constant of the homosexual experience (Anthony Heilbut, one of Mann's many biographers, refers to the novelist's specific brand of homosexual erotics as 'inherently asymmetrical, linking the wise and ugly with the beautiful dummies'), it has retained its position at the pinnacle of gay literature, of what might whimsically be defined as 'homotextuality'.

There have, to be sure, existed potential rivals to Mann's eminence as a chronicler of homosexual desire, yet not one of them has proved to be, for various reasons, wholly satisfactory.

Gide, for example. Even if he married, except that it was a *mariage blanc*, and fathered a daughter, except that it was not his long-suffering wife's, he was not only an unrepentant homosexual but the first major twentieth-century writer to declare himself so, relating in a notorious confessional passage how, in North Africa, he was confronted with the truth of his sexual nature by no less a mentor than Wilde. He even wrote a Socratic apologia of inversion, *Corydon*, an eccentric book that led to the inscription of his complete works on the now defunct Catholic Index. Yet, because his sexual orientation was what we would think of today as paedophiliac, none of his tireless proselytising has enabled him to jump posterity's queue, so to speak. No gay rights campaigners have ever cited the pioneering example of André Gide. Once a pillar of the Index, all he can hope for any longer, at least outside his native land, is to make an appearance in the index of someone else's biography.

What, then, about Proust? Although no closeted homosexual in his private life, and although arguably the finest novelist of the twentieth (or any) century, in whose multi-volume masterpiece a quite astounding, not to say statistically implausible, number of characters are revealed to be deviants, Proust was himself, alas, a hypocrite in so far as his public attitude to homosexuality was concerned. Not only was he prepared to alter genders in *A la recherche du temps perdu* in craven conformity to the prevailing social orthodoxy – most famously that of Albertine, whose fickle relationship with the Narrator was inspired by Proust's own jealous liaison with his chauffeur, Albert Agostino – but he portrayed almost all his gay characters as parasitical wastrels fit only for the dustbins of history. (The disturbing absence in the novel of any sense of authorial *sympathy* for homosexuality was the primary cause of Gide's subsequently regretted criticism of the *Recherche*.) And, philistine as it may appear, there is also the off-putting fact, particularly for contemporary readers, that, unlike Mann's svelte novella, Proust's novel runs to several dense volumes. In an age as pressurised as ours, an age in which everything tends to impress us as *too long* (a biography at five hundred pages, a film at two hours, a soundbite at twenty words), who has time to read a *roman-fleuve* about Time?

Who else? Cocteau? He has been generally dismissed (as already was the case with Wilde, at least prior to his posthumous beatification) as too flighty, too precious, too much the flibbertigibbet, to be co-opted as a universal role model – an image not helped, among the gay community, by the fact that, apart from in one anonymously published text, *Le Livre blanc* (*The White Paper*), he never once dared to write with any candour about homosexuality, his own or anyone else's. Even in his posthumous diaries, he continued to allude to his lovers as his 'sons', even his 'adopted sons', as though he were hoping to cheat posterity, to cheat God.

Genet? A thief, a bruiser, a rhapsodist of rough trade, not everyone's cup of tea. Forster? He was the kind of homosexual the Brits have always preferred, stoically buttoned-up and consumed by guilt, whose sole gay-themed novel, *Maurice*, complete with deliriously happy ending, is incompetent both as fiction and as wishful thinking. Isherwood? His single most memorable creation was, unfortunately, a heterosexual woman, the 'Sally Bowles' of the Berlin stories. Gore Vidal? Too patrician and narcissistic, too jowly and smug. Mishima? Too Japanese.

There thus remains Mann; and it must be said that, for all its apparent irrelevancies to a modern gay readership, it's not hard to understand how appealing *Death in Venice* remains to such a constituency. The planet has its erogenous zones and, for homosexuals, Venice, that rancid pop-up book of a city compared by Cocteau to 'an amorous negress lying dead in her bath with all her tawdry jewels', has always been one of them, a rich breeding ground of (in the biological sense) sterile love.

It was the eighteenth-century art historian Johann Winckelmann who did most to promote Italian beauty as not only an aesthetic but a sexual ideal. Although his works are now certainly little read, he pioneered the vogue for neoclassicism and laid the foundations of modern art criticism and connoisseurship, thereby providing a useful gloss of cultural respectability for 'the homosexual diaspora', that southwards drift, as if by a gravitational force, of affluent gay northern Europeans, principally Germans, English and French. Winckelmann was a homosexual himself (he was murdered in 1768 in mysterious circumstances) whose aesthetic credo was intimately linked, as would be the case again and again in the years to come, with his erotic fantasies. His ideal, both sculpturally and sexually, in marble as in flesh, was a just-pubescent youth ('it was with an almost audible smack of the lips that he referred to the athletes at Olympia or dilated on the beauty of marble genitals,' wrote Hugh Honour, the historian of neoclassicism); and this ideal, disseminated through his own writings, as well as those of Platen, Byron, Pater, Housman, Wilde and Corvo, remained crucial to the homosexual cult of the ephebe up to and including, precisely, the Tadzio of *Death in Venice* (who, although Polish, has his blond northern pallor subsumed in the hot and heady aura of the city in which Aschenbach encounters him).

There was what might be called a push-and-pull

factor to this wilful self-exile: push, being the wish
or obligation to quit one's own country; pull, the
almost inevitable decision to settle in Italy. Homosexuals left their northern homelands for one basic
reason, the fact that, in both Britain and Germany,
the principal points of departure, homosexuality was
until relatively recently a criminal offence. They tended to gravitate towards the Mediterranean, however,
for several reasons. Because of a craving to escape
Northern Europe's manic-depressive weather. Because
life in Italy was ridiculously inexpensive. Because,
more contentiously, young male Italians were said to
attain sexual maturity three or four years before boys
further north. Because, too, the sexual inclinations of
these boys were famously 'catholic', unconstrained
by gender loyalties. (According to a certain Dr. A.
Sper, author of a not entirely disinterested pamphlet
on *Capri und die Homosexuellen*, which was published in 1902, 'one has only to show an interest in a
halfgrown youth, to remark on his curly hair or his
almond-shaped eyes, and the young man begins to
flirt'.) Because Naples, Capri and Venice all had a
history of institutionalised paedophilia (the Emperor
Tiberius was fond of filling his Capriote swimming-
pool with 'minnows'). And, not least, because erudite
homosexuals had read their Virgil and Theocritus and

felt able to legitimise their escapades by inscribing them within a noble and civilised tradition of classico-pastoral dalliance.

By the turn and teens of the last century, however, the Grand Tour having surrendered to a rather ungrand tourism, the classical analogy was coming under strain. It was increasingly difficult to imagine oneself as a contemporary, white-suited, Panama-hatted Zeus descending among the mortals to bear off some cute Ganymede when the monetary aspect of the affair, present even in Winckelmann's time, had become so conspicuous. And when the action eventually switched to Taormina, where the Baron von Gloeden, amateur photographer and pornographer, the Mapplethorpe of his day, set up his tripod, grafting the poses and props of a conventional, codified Antiquity on to the grubby, proletarian bodies of gap-toothed Sicilian gigolos, the whole thing risked subsiding into near-farcical kitsch.

What, if anything, nowadays remains of that once haughty (and also, of course, hypocritical) ideal? What else but the rapacious sexual tourism which drives European paedophiles ever further southwards to purchase their even younger, even poorer, even cheaper Ganymedes in such 'gay paradises' as Sri Lanka, Thailand and the Philippines. At least, no one any longer could describe the trade as hypocritical.

The significance, then, of *Death in Venice* in the sociocultural history of homosexuality is that, while, on the one hand, it represented the last gasp, the last legitimate squeak, of the neoclassical mytho-iconography which had long permitted Europe's wealthy, cultivated inverts to encode and sublimate their sexual nature in the archetypes of classical poetry, it constituted, too, that same mythology's ironic critique. Although it has been much-derided (particularly in Visconti's film version, which had two parallel rivulets of mascara running from Bogarde's tear-welling eyes), the novella's closing sequence, of Aschenbach's slow death on the Lido as he observes a semi-naked Tadzio posing before the sleeping sea, beckoning him towards 'an immensity rich with unutterable expectation', was not at all, on Mann's part, a lamentable lapse in taste. An ideal had expired, and it was necessary for Zeus to be exposed at last for what he also, always, had been, even in his pristine mythological heyday: a dirty old man.

What, then, renders Mann's masterpiece so enduringly seductive is above all what one of his translators, David Luke, has defined as its 'striking fusion of realism and concrete symbolism', the bizarre admixture in its linguistic style of high-toned classicism and pervasive if just hinted-at raunchiness, coupled with the equally bizarre admixture, in its narrative textures and trappings, of the psychological case-history and the mythological romance.

***

And the last word?

In modern Hollywood the successful launch of a new production is often contingent on the previous success of its director's or writer's original 'pitch'. What precisely is a pitch? Immortalised in Robert Altman's film *The Player*, the term refers to the pre-production session between the so-called creative artists and the financial backers when the former must persuade the latter, *in no more than a single sentence*, of the commercial viability of their project.

The implication of such a pitch – that, if a movie's narrative cannot be encapsulated in a mere dozen words, then it cannot hope to pack them in at the multiplexes – is universally, and for the most part justifiably, regarded outside Hollywood as one of the most blatant signifiers of the American film industry's ineradicable philistinism.

And yet... And yet... Consider the following pitches. A one-legged sea captain sacrifices himself in his obsessive pursuit of a great white whale. A man wakes up one morning to discover that, overnight, he has been transformed into a cockroach. A young king, attempting to learn why his kingdom is blighted by a plague, arrives at the horrified realisation that he has murdered his own father and married his own mother. Or – and the reader will doubtless have seen me coming – a prestigious German writer is enticed to his death in a cholera-stricken Venice by his undeclared and unrequited passion for an exquisitely beautiful Polish boy.

It would be absurd to claim that a novel or even a novella is valueless if its 'essence' cannot be conveyed in a dozen words. Exceptions are, as they say, legion. Yet, beyond its current status as the homosexual's *Tristan and Isolde*, beyond even its formal perfection, there can surely be little doubt that, just as Mann himself implied when describing his role in the story's gestation as less that of creator than that of recording agent, organising a sequence of partially factual events rather than a sequence of totally fictional imaginings, the unforgettability of *Death in Venice* derives supremely from the fact that its premise is one of the great, simple pitches of world literature.

No human life, though, will ever boast the shapeliness and legibility conducive to a pitch. Lives twist and turn, they are full of narrative split ends, they double back on themselves, they leave far too many dangling, unknotted strands, they tend to be nothing but a tissue of longueurs and langueurs interrupted by the occasional event of import and interest, and they are honeycombed with coincidences so outrageous that all but the trashiest or most inept of novelists would reject them as unworthy of any serious, self-respecting work of fiction.

Such, as we have seen, was the life of Wladyslaw Moes. It can perhaps be done justice to in a short book. Like most people's lives, it could never be pitched.

Wladyslaw Moes, 1900 - 1986

Acknowledgements

The author would like to express his deepest gratitude to
Maria Tarchalski, especially, and to Wojciech Fudakowski
for having shared their memories with him.

About the Author

Gilbert Adair has written five novels, *The Holy Innocents* (which is soon to be filmed by Bernardo Bertolucci), *Love and Death on Long Island* (filmed by Richard Kwietniowski), *The Death of the Author*, *The Key of the Tower* and *A Closed Book*, as well as a full-length verse parody of Alexander Pope, *The Rape of the Cock*, and two sequels to classics of children's literature, *Alice Through the Needle's Eye* and *Peter Pan and the Only Children*. His non-fiction includes *Hollywood's Vietnam* and four collections of essays on cultural themes, *Myths & Memories*, *The Postmodernist Always Rings Twice*, *Flickers* and *Surfing the Zeitgeist*. He won the Scott-Moncrieff Prize for *A Void*, his virtuoso translation of Georges Perec's e-less novel *La Disparition*. He lives in London and is frequently published as a journalist.